Sally

Lehrwerk für den
Englischunterricht ab Klasse 1

Pupil's Book 3

Erarbeitet von
Jasmin Brune
Daniela Elsner
Stefanie Gleixner-Weyrauch
Marion Lugauer
Sabine Schwarz

Auf der Grundlage der Ausgabe von
Martina Bredenbröcker, Jasmin Brune,
Daniela Elsner, Barbara Gleich,
Stefanie Gleixner-Weyrauch,
Simone Gutwerk, Marion Lugauer,
Sabine Schwarz, Anke Spangenberg

Unter Beratung von
Jane Brockmann-Fairchild

Illustriert von
Barbara Jung, Wilfried Poll,
Anja Boretzki, Gisela Vogel

Oldenbourg Schulbuchverlag, München

Inhalt

The happy kangaroo song

1 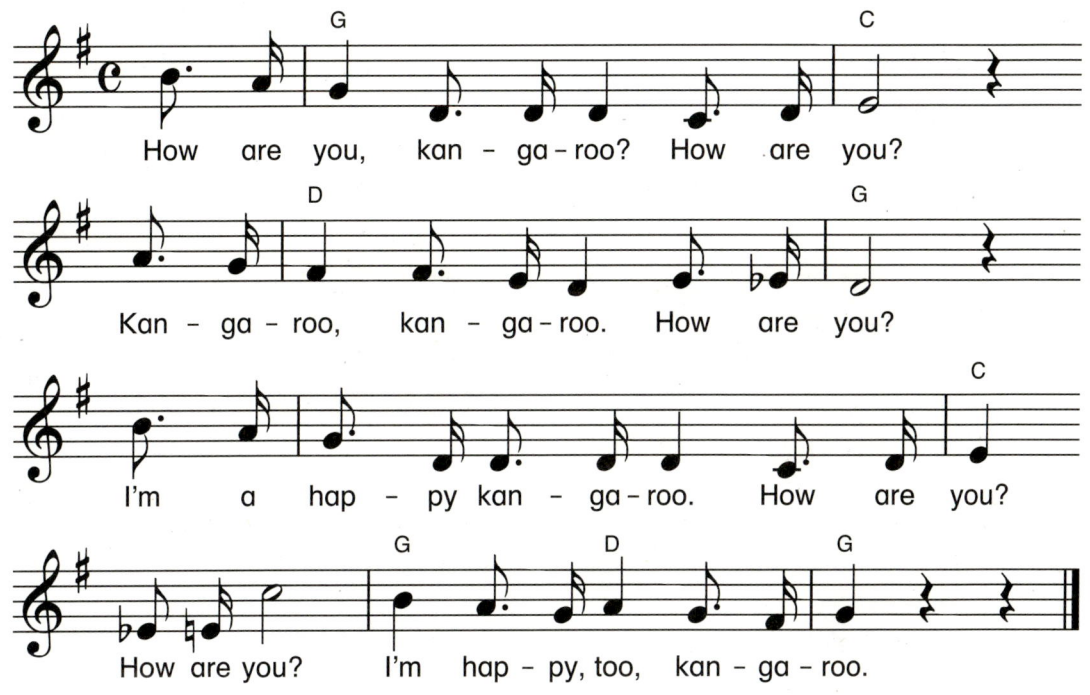 **Listen and sing.**

How are you, kan-ga-roo? How are you?

Kan-ga-roo, kan-ga-roo. How are you?

I'm a hap-py kan-ga-roo. How are you?

How are you? I'm hap-py, too, kan-ga-roo.

2 **Ask your partner:** What's your name? How are you?

What's your name?

My name is Sally.

I'm fine, thanks.

How are you?

English all around

1 There are many English words in the picture.
Look and say: I can see …

2 Make a poster with English words.
Cut out pictures or words from magazines.

⭐ Group the words (sports, food, drinks, …).

Mr Blue and Mrs Yellow

1 🔘 **Listen and point.**

Mr [blue] sees Mrs [yellow].

Hello, Mrs Yellow.

Hello, Mr Blue.

Mr [blue] and Mrs [yellow].

Now Mr [blue] is Mr [green] and Mrs [yellow] is Mrs [green].

2 💬 **What colour is it?**

grey

pink

orange

purple

brown

green

3 👦👧 **Act out the story with a partner.**

Sally's rhyme

1 🔊💬 **Listen, say the rhyme and do the actions.**

One, two, three –
Sally, point to me!

Four, five, six –
Sally, let us mix!

Seven, eight, nine –
now let's stand in line!

Now comes ten,
let's say the rhyme again!

2 💬 **Learn the rhyme.**

In class

1 🔘 **Listen and point.**

pencil
pencil case
ruler
pen
book
schoolbag

MY favourite book

Look at the board.

I've got an orange ruler.

Eric   Phil

Emily

Tim

Liz

Sally

Susan

I've got =
I have got

2 👦👧 **What school things have you got?**
Tell your partner: I've got a ...

⭐ **Make your own picture dictionary.**
Draw and write.

pen

School in England

1 Talk about the photos.

in class

pupils in school uniform

lunchtime

a lollipop lady

2 Listen and read.

Hello, my name is Ella. I'm 9.
I go to Westminster School. I'm in class 3 c.
My teacher is Mrs Black.
My school uniform is red and white.
School starts at 9 o'clock in the morning
and ends at 4 o'clock in the afternoon.
My favourite subjects are music and sports.
What about you?

3 What about your school day? Do a presentation.

Head and shoulders

1 Sing the song and do the actions.

2 Sing the song faster and faster.

3 Sing and drop the word [head].
Sing again and drop the words [head] and [shoulders] ...

Hm and shoulders, knees ...

Hm and hm, knees ...

one knee –
two knee**s**

Ouch!

1 Read the comic.

Snakes and ladders

1 It's your turn. Play the game and do the actions.

FINISH

START

It's my turn.

Roll the dice. Do the actions.

 Correct action 😊 : Go up the ladder.

 Wrong action 🙁 : Go down the snake.

Sally's hotspot:

Correct action 😊 : Roll the dice again.

Wrong action 🙁 : Go back to the start.

 one foot – two feet

3 Touch your head.

8 Bend your knees.

16 Sing: Head and shoulders …

19 Wash your hands.

24 Count your fingers.

27 Shake your feet.

29 Stretch your arms.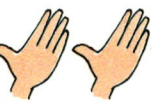

33 Point to your eyes.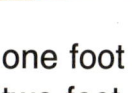

43 Touch your ears.

48 Stretch your legs.

52 Brush your hair.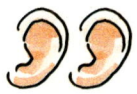

58 Say: Good morning!

59 Point to your nose.

62 Shake your body.

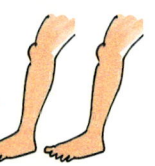

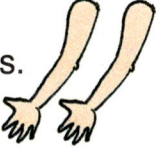

Monster, monster how do you feel?

I'm happy
because my hair is cool.

I'm angry
because a dog ate my chocolate.

I'm scared
because a spider is in my shoe.

I'm sad
because my favourite T-shirt
is too small.

I'm tired
because I chased a ghost all night.

1 Listen and read.

I'm happy because
I have got a lollipop.

Tim's wish list

spaceship £17

£20 helicopter ✗

castle £80

£10 doll

helmet £90 bike

£30

helmet £40 ✗

£100 £200

bike ✗

£18

racing car

football £8

£5 book

£1 rubber

£2 ruler

£3 pencils ✗

1 **Look at the toys. What does Tim want?**
Tell your partner:
Tim wants to have a bike …

2 **Ask your partner:** How much is the …?

3 **Make a wish list for your class and discuss.**
We want to have …

I want –
Tim want**s**

The fish who could wish

In the deep blue sea, in the deep of the blue,
swam a fish who could wish, and each wish would come true.

He wished for a castle.

He wished for a car.

He wished for a horse and a Spanish guitar.

One day, just for fun, that silly old fish,
wished the silliest, silliest wish he could wish.

That silly old fish wished he could be
just like all the other fish in the sea.

But wishing was something other fish could not do.
So that was his very last wish that came true.

1 🔘 **Listen and point.**

2 👦👧 **Look at the pictures.
Tell the story to your partner.**

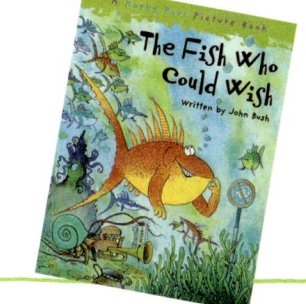

Sally in the snow

Sally, it's cold!

Sally, it's cold!!!

1 **Listen and point.**

T-shirt

socks

trousers

pullover

boots

jacket

scarf

woolly hat

gloves

Rrring!

Hi, Sally!

Hello!

2 🗨 **Look and say:** Sally put**s** on her …
Sally take**s** off her …

3 **Do the clothes rally.**

What's the weather like?

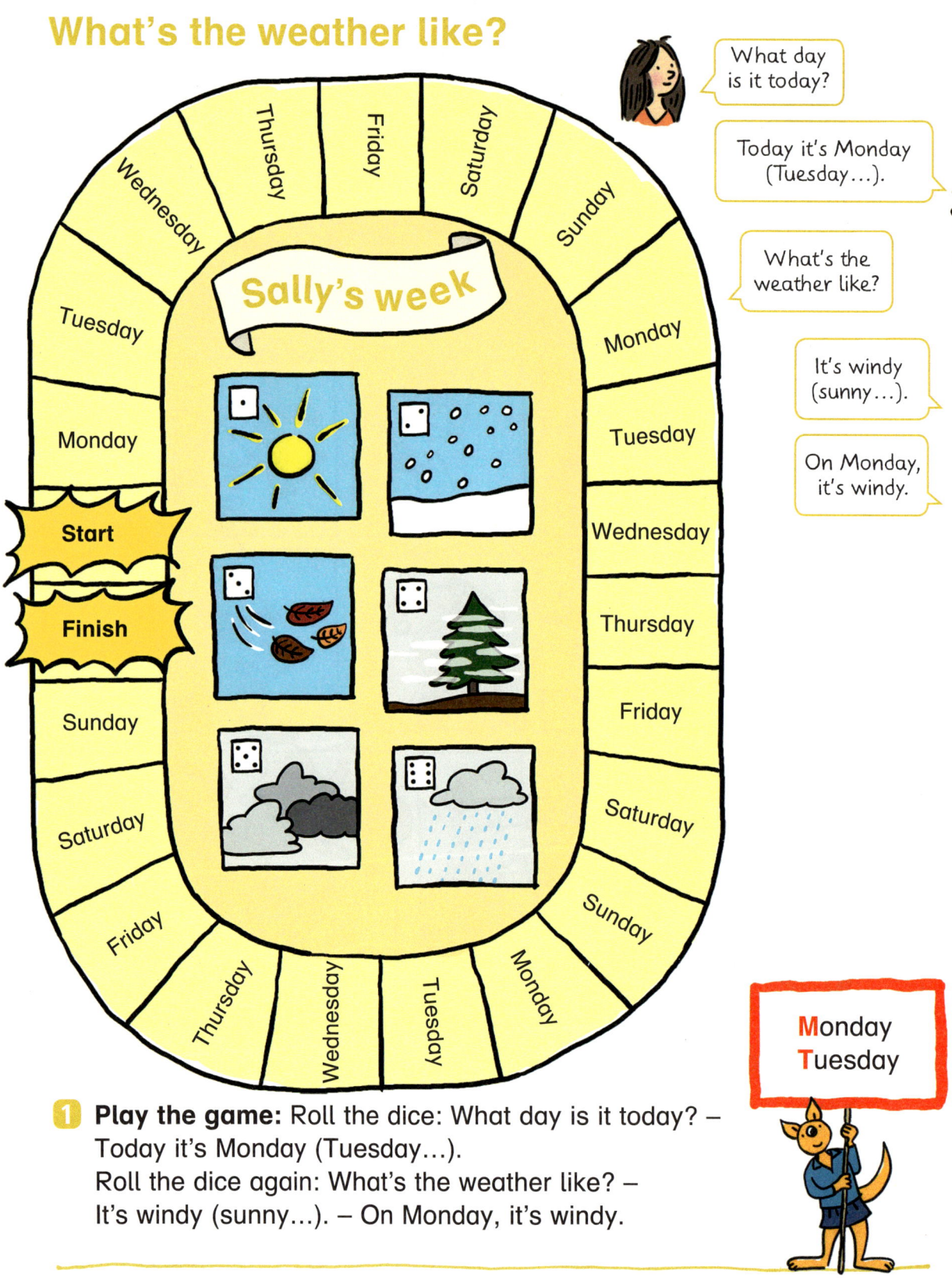

What day is it today?

Today it's Monday (Tuesday…).

What's the weather like?

It's windy (sunny…).

On Monday, it's windy.

Monday
Tuesday

1 **Play the game:** Roll the dice: What day is it today? –
Today it's Monday (Tuesday…).
Roll the dice again: What's the weather like? –
It's windy (sunny…). – On Monday, it's windy.

The wind and the sun

1 Look at the picture. What can you see?

2 Listen to the story. Tell it to your partner.

3 Act out the story in your group.

The weather forecast

London
Berlin
Rome
Istanbul

snowy

foggy

LONDON

BERLIN

windy, rainy

sunny

ROME

ISTANBUL

Today it's
…

What's the
weather like
today?

1 Talk about the picture.

2 What's the weather like? Listen, point and tell.

3 What's the weather like in Paris, in Hamburg …?
Look in a newspaper or on the Internet.
Make a weather forecast in your group
and do a presentation.

⭐ Make a weather chart for one week.

Presentation tips:
• Speak loudly and clearly.
• Look at the class.
• Show pictures.

Happy birthday

Birthday invitation

Dear Susan,
Please come to my birthday party.

When: Saturday, 5 March at 2 o'clock
Where: 25, Main Street
Phone: 3472

Can you come to my party?
Yours, Emily

January	February	March
		5 Emily
April	May	June
July	August	September
October	November	December

HAPPY BIRTHDAY

1 Make a birthday calendar.

2 Talk about Emily's birthday party.

3 How do you celebrate your birthday?
Tell your class.

4 Write a birthday invitation.

January
February

Keith Haring

the artist

"Best buddies"

"Football"

"Group"

1 Look at the pictures.
Describe the colours and actions.

group work

presentation

"Dancing in the sun"

"Friends"

2 **Make a picture about friends:**
1. Cut out different figures.
2. Glue them on coloured paper.
3. Trace your figures with a black pen.

My family

my mum and dad

My brother Tim
is 9 years old!

my grandma and grandpa

Can you find my grandma
and grandpa?

This is my aunt.
Her name is
Helen.

Can you find my mum
and Tim?

This is my
family!

How old is Susan?

1 **Look and point.**

2 **What about your family? Tell.**

What is it?

tea, coke, orange juice, coffee, hot chocolate, milk

1 💬 **Look and guess.**

At the drinks stand

2 **Look and read.**

3 **Make your own drinks stand. Act out the scene.**

4 **Make a poster about drinks.**

The magic trick

1 Do the trick.

2 Can you do a magic trick? Show your class.

1 orange juice
2 honey
3 tea
4 toast
5 ham
6 water
7 bread
8 hot chocolate
9 jam
10 cheese
11 egg
12 coffee
13 milk
14 roll
15 cornflakes

My favourite breakfast

everyday breakfast

traditional cooked breakfast

1 💬 **Look and speak.**

2 **Ask your partner.**

3 **What do you have for breakfast?**
For breakfast, I have …

4 **Do the breakfast rally.**

 **Fruit**

At the ice cream stand

Can I help you?

banana
cherry
pear
vanilla
chocolate
lemon
strawberry
orange
pineapple

Let's have an ice cream.

I'd like …

1 cherr**y** –
2 cherr**ie**s

1 Listen and speak.

2 **Ask your partner:** What's your favourite ice cream?

⭐ **Find more nouns ending with y. Build the plural.**

Let's make a smoothie

1 **Look and read.**

This is what you need.

Wash the strawberries.

Peel the bananas.

Cut the fruit.

Put them into the jug.

Add water or milk.

Mix it.

Pour the smoothie into your glass.

Enjoy!

2 **Make your own smoothie.**

  **Pets**

Little dog lost

 Listen. Where is Bobby?

These pets have new homes

dog

Jack and Mr Tailor

rabbit

Hopsy and Sophie Miller

cat

Tippy and Mrs Davis

guinea pig

Molly and Kevin Fisher

hamster

Fred and Alice Smith

tortoise

Rocky and Sammy Baker

budgie

Charlie and Mrs Cooper

1 Listen, look and speak.

2 Make a missing pet report.

3 Act it out with your partner.

mouse   Speedy

100 little kangaroos are sitting on Big Ben

100 little kangaroos are sitting on Big Ben.
10 of them just jump away. How many are there then?

90 little kangaroos are sitting on Big Ben.
10 of them just jump away. How many are there then?

80 little kangaroos are sitting on Big Ben.
10 of them just jump away. How many are there then?

70 little kangaroos are sitting on Big Ben.
10 of them just jump away. How many are there then?
…

1 🔊 **Listen and sing.**

2 **Sing the song faster and faster.**

twenty, thirty, forty, …

Let's go to London!

the Royal Family

guards

Buckingham Palace

Tower Bridge

the London Eye

Big Ben

1 Look at the photos.

2 Make a poster about London sights.

I want to be a queen!

Clumsy the dog

At night …

The next morning …

Who stole the eggs?

Clumsy, was that you?

Me? No, it wasn't me. Not this time!

But Clumsy, you always say that.

In the evening …

CLUMSY

It wasn't me … Why don't they believe me?

The next morning …

Wake up! It wasn't Clumsy. Look!

Hold the thief!

Clumsy, good thing you are so clumsy!

Oops!

1 Listen to the story.

2 Read the story.

Alphabet rhyme

A B C D E F G,
on the farm there is a bee.

H I J K L M N,
it lands directly on a hen.

How
are you?

O P Q R S T U,
and asks her friendly:
"How are you?"

Get off my
head!

V W X Y Z,
"I'm fine, but please,
get off my head."

1 Listen and point.

2 Read the rhyme.

3 Do the animal rally.

On the beach

She sells seashells on the seashore.

1 💬 **Look and speak. How many seashells can you find?**

2 🐕 **Create your own summer exhibition in groups.
Use your dictionary. Present it to your class.**

Robin Hood's game

The game board shows a path from START to 26 winding through Sherwood Forest.

Text on the game board:
- Take the sheriff's clothes. Go to 16.
- You want to have a drink. Miss a turn.
- Ride a horse. Go to 11.
- Get your arrows. Go to 1.
- Nottingham
- START

Numbered spaces: 1, 2, 3, 4, 5, 6, 7, 8, 9, 10, 11, 12, 13, 14, 15, 24, 25, 26

1 Play the game.

Robin Hood

Look!
The sheriff is coming.
Go to 16.

17

18

19

You want to
have breakfast
on the farm.
Miss a turn.

20

Wave to the farmer.
Go to 37.

34

35

36

33

37

21

22

3

Hide
behind
the tree.
Go to 19.

32

Drink some milk.
Go to 34.

38

k at
castle.
the dice again.

31

39

30

40

29

28

41

7

Give money to the poor.
Go to 31.

42

FINISH

Rush hour

The ghost

I saw a ghost.
He saw me, too.
I waved at him.
But he said "Boo!".

Boo!

Tongue twister

Two witches are watching two watches.
Which witch is watching which watch?

1 💬 **Look and read.**
Can you say the tongue twister?

⭐ **Choose a witch and describe her to your partner.**

It's Halloween

1 Listen to the song.

2 Listen to the story.

Act out the story.

Christmas Eve

1 **Look and find these Christmas things:**
mistletoe, Christmas tree, stockings, Christmas cards, presents

2 Listen to the story.

3 How do you celebrate Christmas?

I hear them

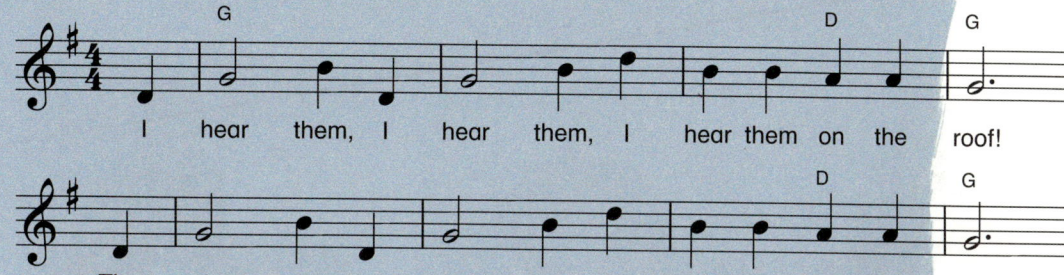

I hear them, I hear them, I hear them on the roof!

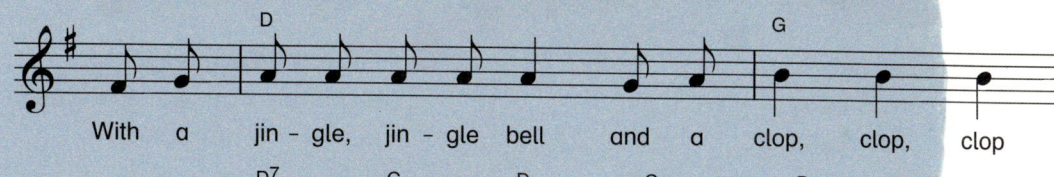

The rein – deer are com – ing, I hear each pranc – ing hoof!

With a jin – gle, jin – gle bell and a clop, clop, clop

and a clat – ter, clat – ter, clat – ter at the chim – ney top.

I hear them, I hear them, I hear them on the roof!

I wish you a Merry Christmas and a Happy New Year.

1. Listen to the song.

2. Sing the song.

3. Act out the song.

4. Make a Christmas card.

Make your own Christmas stocking

You need:
thick brown paper, a pencil,
scissors, glue, a hole punch,
wool, felt tips or wax crayons
and coloured paper

1

Draw a large stocking
on the thick brown paper.
Cut out two copies of the stocking.

2

3

Glue the two stockings
together around the edges.
Leave the top open.

4

Punch holes around the edges
of the stocking.
Weave wool in and out of the holes.

5

6

Leave a loop of wool
at one end.
Tie it into a knot.
Decorate your stocking.

1 **Look and read.**

2 **Create your own stocking.**

⭐ **Describe your stocking.**

Valentine's cards

1 **Read the comic.**

2 **Read the rhymes. What's your favourite rhyme?**

In February
it's Valentine's Day.
I write Valentine's cards
to my friends.

Candy is sweet,
this is true,
but for my Valentine
I'll choose you.

I like you!
Be my Valentine!

Jingle, jangle,
silver bangle,
you look fit
from every angle.

Roses are red,
violets are blue,
sugar is sweet
and so are you!

3  **Make your own Valentine's card.**

Edgar's Easter eggs

1 🔘 **Listen to the story. Act it out.**

2 💬 **Where are the Easter eggs? Look and tell.**

3 **Look and read.**

You need:
a toilet roll, white paper, pink paper,
glue, scissors, felt tips or coloured pencils,
pipe cleaners

Cover the toilet roll
with white paper.

Draw a bunny face
on it.

Cut out two ears from the
white paper and the centres
from the pink paper.

Glue on the ears.

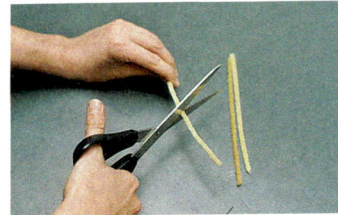

Glue on the
pipe cleaners.

4 **Make your own Easter egg cup.**

Hello   Hallo

boy   Junge
girl   Mädchen
children   Kinder

basketball   Basketball
computer game   Computerspiel
inline skating   Inlineskaten
singing   Singen
skateboard   Skateboard
tennis   Tennis

Hello./Hi.   Hallo.

Good morning.   Guten Morgen.

How are you? – I'm fine, thanks.
Wie geht es dir? – Danke, gut.

What's your name? – My name is …
Wie heißt du? – Ich heiße …

What do you like? –
I like … And you?
Was magst du? –
Ich mag … Und du?

I can see (a) …   Ich sehe (ein/e) …

 Colours and numbers
Farben und Zahlen

black   schwarz
blue   blau
brown   braun
green   grün
grey   grau
orange   orange
pink   rosa, pink
purple   lila
red   rot

white   weiß
yellow   gelb

one   eins
two   zwei
three   drei
four   vier
five   fünf
six   sechs
seven   sieben
eight   acht
nine   neun
ten   zehn

What colour is it? –
It's green (blue …).
Welche Farbe hat es? –
Es ist grün (blau …).

What's your telephone number? –
My telephone number is …
Wie lautet deine Telefonnummer? –
Meine Telefonnummer ist …

 At school   In der Schule

(black)board   Tafel
book   Buch
class   Klasse
classroom   Klassenzimmer
computer   Computer
folder   Ordner
glue stick   Klebestift
lollipop lady   Schülerlotsin
pen   Füller
pencil   Bleistift
pencil case   Federmäppchen
pencil sharpener   Spitzer
pupil   Schüler, Schülerin

rubber Radiergummi

ruler Lineal

school Schule

schoolbag Schultasche

school things Schulsachen

school uniform Schuluniform

(a pair of) scissors eine Schere

teacher Lehrer, Lehrerin

in in

on auf

under unter

I've got a … Ich habe ein(e, en) …

I go to Westminster School.
Ich gehe in die Westminster-Schule.

I'm in class 3c.
Ich bin in der Klasse 3c.

My teacher is Mrs/Mr …
Meine Lehrerin / Mein Lehrer
heißt Frau/Herr …

 Body and feelings
Körper und Gefühle

arm Arm

body Körper

ear Ohr

eye Auge

face Gesicht

finger Finger

foot – feet Fuß – Füße

hair Haar

hand Hand

head Kopf

knee Knie

leg Bein

mouth Mund

nose Nase

shoulder Schulter

toe Zeh

tooth – teeth Zahn – Zähne

angry zornig

fine gut

happy glücklich

sad traurig

scared verängstigt, erschrocken

tired müde

How do you feel? – I'm happy/sad …
I feel …
Wie fühlst du dich? – Ich bin
glücklich/traurig …

I'm okay. Mir geht's ganz gut.

 Toys Spielzeug

big groß

car Auto

castle Burg, Schloss

children Kinder

computer game Computerspiel

doll Puppe

fish Fisch

football Fußball

guitar Gitarre

helicopter Hubschrauber

helmet Helm

horse Pferd

bike Fahrrad

racing car Rennauto

small klein

spaceship Raumschiff

teddy bear Teddybär

(to) want wollen

(to) wish (for) sich wünschen

eleven   elf

twelve   zwölf

thirteen   dreizehn

fourteen   vierzehn

fifteen   fünfzehn

sixteen   sechzehn

seventeen   siebzehn

eighteen   achtzehn

nineteen   neunzehn

twenty   zwanzig

British   britisch

money   Geld

penny – pence (p)   Penny – Pence

pound (£)   Pfund

How much is the ...? –
The ... is ... pounds.
Wie viel kostet der (die, das) ...? –
Der (die, das) ... kostet ... Pfund.

How much is it? – It's ... pounds.   Wie
viel kostet das? – Das macht ... Pfund.

Tim/Susan wants ...
Tim/Susan möchte ...

Clothes   Kleidung

boots   Stiefel

cap   Kappe

coat   Mantel

dress   Kleid

gloves   Handschuhe

jacket   Jacke

(a pair of) jeans   eine Jeans

pullover   Pullover

(to) put on   anziehen

scarf   Schal

shirt   Hemd

shoes   Schuhe

(a pair of) shorts
eine kurze Hose, Shorts

skirt   Rock

socks   Socken

(to) take off   ausziehen

(a pair of) trousers   eine Hose

T-shirt   T-Shirt

(to) wear   tragen, anhaben

woolly hat   Mütze

For my holidays, I pack ...
Für meine Ferien packe ich ... ein.

Sally puts on her ... / takes off her ...
Sally zieht ihr(e, en) ... an/aus.

Weather and days
Wetter und Tage

Monday   Montag

Tuesday   Dienstag

Wednesday   Mittwoch

Thursday   Donnerstag

Friday   Freitag

Saturday   Samstag

Sunday   Sonntag

day   Tag

week   Woche

cloud/y   Wolke/wolkig

cold   kalt

fog/gy   Nebel/neblig

hot   heiß

rain/y   Regen/regnerisch

snow/y   Schnee/verschneit

sun/ny   Sonne/sonnig

weather forecast   Wettervorhersage

wind/y   Wind/windig

When can we meet? – We can meet on Monday (Tuesday …). Wann können wir uns treffen? – Wir können uns am Montag (Dienstag …) treffen.

What day is it today? – Today it's Monday. (Tuesday ...). Welchen Tag haben wir heute? – Es ist Montag (Dienstag ...).

What's the weather like? – It's windy (sunny …). Wie ist das Wetter? – Es ist windig (sonnig …).

On Monday, it's sunny. Am Montag ist es sonnig.

Around the year
Rund ums Jahr

January Januar
February Februar
March März
April April
May Mai
June Juni
July Juli
August August
September September
October Oktober
November November
December Dezember
month Monat

spring Frühling
summer Sommer
autumn Herbst
winter Winter
season Jahreszeit

balloon Ballon
birthday Geburtstag
cake Torte, Kuchen
calendar Kalender
candle Kerze
card Karte
crown Krone
guest Gast
invitation Einladung
party Party, Feier
present Geschenk

When's your birthday? – My birthday is in … Wann ist dein Geburtstag? – Mein Geburtstag ist im …

Happy birthday! Alles Gute zum Geburtstag!

How old are you? – I'm eight (years old). Wie alt bist du? – Ich bin acht (Jahre alt).

Family and friends
Familie und Freunde

aunt Tante
boy Junge
brother Bruder
family Familie
father/dad Vater/Papa
friend Freund(in)
girl Mädchen
grandfather/grandpa Großvater/Opa
grandmother/grandma Großmutter/Oma
mother/mum Mutter/Mama
sister Schwester
uncle Onkel

My best friend is ...
Mein(e) beste(r) Freund(in) ist ...

He/She is ... years old.
Er/Sie ist ... Jahre alt.

He/She has got ...   Er/Sie hat ...

Have you got brothers or sisters? –
I've got ... / I haven't got ...
Hast du Geschwister? –
Ich habe ... / Ich habe keine ...

This is my family. /
These are my friends.
Das ist meine Familie. /
Dies sind meine Freunde.

 ## Drinks   Getränke

coffee   Kaffee
coke   Cola
hot chocolate   Kakao
lemonade   Limonade
(a glass of) milk   (ein Glas) Milch
orange juice   Orangensaft
(a cup of) tea   (eine Tasse) Tee
water   Wasser

What drinks do you like? – I like ...
Welche Getränke magst du? –
Ich mag ...

I like ... best.   Am liebsten mag ich ...

What drinks don't you like? –
I don't like ...
Welche Getränke magst du nicht? –
Ich mag kein(e, en) ...

What would you like to drink? –
I'd like ..., please.   Was würdest du
gerne trinken? – Ich hätte gerne ..., bitte.

 ## Breakfast   Frühstück

bread   Brot
breakfast   Frühstück
butter   Butter
cheese   Käse
cornflakes   Cornflakes
(to) drink   trinken
(to) eat   essen
egg   Ei
ham   Schinken
honey   Honig
jam   Marmelade
roll   Brötchen
toast   Toast

What do you have for breakfast?
Was isst/trinkst du zum Frühstück?

For breakfast, I have ...
Zum Frühstück esse/trinke ich ...

Do you like ...? –
Yes, I do. / No, I don't.
Magst du ...? – Ja. / Nein.

Can I have the ..., please? –
Here you are.   Kann ich bitte den/die/
das ... haben? – Hier, bitte.

 ## Fruit   Obst

apple   Apfel
banana   Banane
cherry   Kirsche
fruit   Frucht, Obst
lemon   Zitrone
melon   Melone
orange   Orange, Apfelsine
pear   Birne

Words

pineapple Ananas
plum Pflaume
strawberry Erdbeere
tree Baum

(to) add hinzufügen
(to) cut schneiden
ice cream Eiskrem
ice cream stand Eisstand
jug Krug
(to) mix mischen
(to) peel schälen
(to) pour eingießen
(to) put hineingeben, legen, stellen
scoop Eiskugel
smoothie Smoothie, Fruchtshake
(to) wash waschen

What's your favourite ice cream?
Was ist dein Lieblingseis?

Can I help you?
Kann ich dir/euch/Ihnen helfen?

I'd like … – Here you are.
Ich hätte gerne … – Hier, bitte.

That's … pounds, please. – Thank you.
Das macht bitte … Pfund. – Danke.

Goodbye. Auf Wiedersehen.

Pets Haustiere

bird Vogel
budgie Wellensittich
cat Katze
dog Hund
fish Fisch(e)
guinea pig Meerschweinchen
hamster Hamster

mouse – mice Maus – Mäuse
pet Haustier
rabbit Kaninchen
tail Schwanz
tortoise Schildkröte
wing Flügel

What's your favourite pet?
Was ist dein Lieblingshaustier?

My favourite pet is a …
Mein Lieblingshaustier ist ein(e) …

Its name is … Es heißt …

Can I help you? – I've lost my pet.
Kann ich dir/euch/Ihnen helfen? – Ich
habe mein Haustier verloren.

What colour is it? – It's black
(brown …).
Welche Farbe hat es? – Es ist
schwarz (braun …).

 London London

England England
guard Wache, Wachposten
king König
(to) move bewegen, sich bewegen
palace Palast
prince Prinz
princess Prinzessin
queen Königin
Royal Family Königsfamilie
sight Sehenswürdigkeit

I want to be a … Ich will ein(e) … sein.

I want to see … Ich will … sehen.

Farm animals
Bauernhoftiere

animal   Tier

barn   Stall

bee   Biene

clumsy   ungeschickt

cow   Kuh

duck   Ente

farm   Bauernhof

farmer   Bauer

goose – geese   Gans – Gänse

hen   Huhn, Henne

horse   Pferd

pig   Schwein

sheep   Schaf, Schafe

What's your favourite animal? –
It's a …
Was ist dein Lieblingstier? –
Es ist ein(e) …

Summer   Sommer

airbed   Luftmatratze

beach   Strand

beach ball   Wasserball

(to) build   bauen

holidays   Ferien

ice cream   Eiskrem

(to) play   spielen

sand   Sand

sandcastle   Sandburg

sea   Meer

seashell   Muschel

(to) snorkel   schnorcheln

suncream   Sonnenkrem

sunglasses   Sonnenbrille

(to) swim   schwimmen

towel   Handtuch

How many … can you see/find? –
I can see/find …
Wie viele … kannst du sehen/finden? –
Ich kann … sehen/finden.

Robin Hood   Robin Hood

arrow   Pfeil

bow   Bogen

castle   Burg, Schloss

(to) catch   fangen

(to) dress up   sich verkleiden

forest   Wald

hat   Hut

(to) play a trick

einen Streich spielen

poor   arm

rich   reich

(to) ride (a horse)

(ein Pferd) reiten

sheriff   Sheriff

(to) shoot   schießen

Help!   Hilfe!

Hands up!   Hände hoch!

Happy Halloween
Fröhliches Halloween

bat   Fledermaus

broom   Besen

costume   Kostüm, Verkleidung

dark   dunkel

door   Tür

ghost   Geist, Gespenst

Halloween   Halloween

hat   Hut

house   Haus

(to) knock   klopfen

monster   Ungeheuer, Monster

moon   Mond

night   Nacht

pumpkin   Kürbis

(to) shake   schütteln

skeleton   Gerippe, Skelett

star   Stern

sweets   Süßigkeiten

witch   Hexe

Happy Halloween!
Fröhliches Halloween!

It's eight (nine …) o'clock.
Es ist acht (neun …) Uhr.

Trick or treat!   Süßes oder Saures!

Merry Christmas
Frohe Weihnachten

bell   Glocke

carrot   Karotte

chimney   Schornstein

Christmas card   Weihnachtskarte

Christmas Eve   Heiligabend,
Weihnachtsabend

Christmas tree   Weihnachtsbaum

Father Christmas   Weihnachtsmann

fireplace   (offener) Kamin

(to) get presents   Geschenke
bekommen

mistletoe   Mistel(zweig)

reindeer   Rentier(e)

sleigh   Schlitten

snowman   Schneemann

stocking   Strumpf

Merry Christmas!   Frohe Weihnachten!

Valentine's Day
Valentinstag

Valentine's Day   Valentinstag

(to) write Valentine's cards
Valentinskarten schreiben

It's Valentine's Day.
Es ist Valentinstag.

I like you.   Ich mag dich.

Happy Easter   Frohe Ostern

basket   Korb

bush   Busch

(to) colour   färben, anmalen

Easter bunny   Osterhase

Easter egg   Osterei

Easter egg cup   Ostereierbecher

fence   Zaun

fun   Spaß

happy   glücklich

(to) hide   verstecken

sad   traurig

(to) share   teilen

behind   hinter

in   in

in front of   vor

on   auf

under   unter

Happy Easter!   Frohe Ostern!

Is the yellow (red …) egg in/on/under
the …?
Ist das gelbe (rote …) Ei in/auf/unter
dem/der …?